THE MARKET ADVENTURE

~ by Kristin Cashore ~
illustrated by Janet Nelson

Scott Foresman
is an imprint of

Glenview, Illinois • Boston, Massachusetts • Chandler, Arizona
Upper Saddle River, New Jersey

Photographs

Every effort has been made to secure permission and provide appropriate credit for photographic material. The publisher deeply regrets any omission and pledges to correct errors called to its attention in subsequent editions.

Unless otherwise acknowledged, all photographs are the property of Pearson Education, Inc.

Photo locators denoted as follows: Top (T), Center (C), Bottom (B), Left (L), Right (R), Background (Bkgd)

16 Michele Falzone/Alamy Images.

Illustrations Janet Nelson

ISBN 13: 978-0-328-51370-3
ISBN 10:   0-328-51370-9

7 8 9 10 V0FL 16 15 14 13

"Oh, rats!" Dad said.

Amelia looked into the kitchen. Dad was standing at the counter with Amelia's brother, Ben. They were chopping vegetables.

"What's wrong, Dad?" Amelia asked.

"We forgot to get a chili pepper," Dad said.

"I could run down to the store for one," Amelia said.

Amelia and her family had been living in Mexico for only a week. Amelia's mother was going to teach at a school there for a year.

Amelia and her family lived on the third floor of their building. The supermarket was just down the street. Amelia knew a little Spanish—enough to buy a chili pepper.

"That would be great, Amelia!" Dad said. "Ben, will you go with her?"

"Sure!" said Ben.

Dad gave Amelia some change. Amelia ran down the stairs, and Ben followed. Amelia burst onto the street.

Then she rubbed her eyes. She put her hand against the building to steady herself. She couldn't believe what she was seeing!

Amelia's street was usually peaceful and calm. There weren't many people who lived there. It was a very quiet neighborhood.

But the street had changed! There were hundreds of people walking around. There were big stands made of wood and metal. People were selling all sorts of things at the stands. Her quiet street was noisy and colorful!

Ben stepped into the street behind Amelia. "Wow!" he said. "What's going on?"

Ben and Amelia stood at the edge of the crowd. At a stand nearby, a man arranged pots and pans on a table. He stacked them on top of each other. They wobbled dangerously, but they did not fall.

At another stand, a woman unwrapped bundles of brightly colored cloth. She shook them out so that everyone could see them. Amelia's eyes took in the colors of pink, yellow, green, and orange.

The stands stretched all the way down the street. Amelia could see toys, lamps, shoes, fish, meat, fruits, and vegetables. People walked up and down the street, doing their errands.

"It's an open-air market," Ben said.

"Hey, Ben," Amelia said, "do you think we could buy Dad's chili pepper at this market?"

"I don't see why not," Ben said.

Amelia and Ben stepped into the crowd. They walked past a stand with flowers. They saw a stand with watermelons.

One man stood behind a big pile of carrots and onions. He called out excitedly in Spanish, and Amelia understood him.

"Buy my carrots and onions! I have the best carrots and onions!" he shouted.

Amelia and Ben stopped at a hat stand. A man was buying a big straw hat with a wide brim called a *sombrero*. The hat seller told the man a price.

"No," said the man. "That is too much." The man offered the hat seller a lower price.

"No," said the hat seller. "That is not enough." Then the hat seller told the man a new price. Finally, they agreed. The man paid for the hat and left. He seemed very happy.

"Wow," said Amelia. "I guess at this market you're supposed to bargain for a lower price."

Amelia and Ben kept walking. There were so many sights and sounds. Everyone was talking.

"Everything smells so good!" Amelia said.

"I have never seen so many fruits and vegetables in my life!" Ben said.

Finally they came to a stand piled high with many kinds of peppers. A big, smiling man stood behind a mountain of chili peppers. Amelia was ready to bargain.

"I need one chili pepper," she said in Spanish.

"Only one chili pepper?" asked the man. "That will be ten centavos, please."

Amelia opened her mouth to argue. But then she remembered. The smallest coin in Mexico is ten centavos! Nothing could cost less than that!

"That is a very good price," she said.

"But of course!" said the man.

Amelia gave the man a ten centavos coin. Ben chose a shiny red chili pepper. "*Muchas gracias*!" Ben and Amelia said. "Thank you very much."

Ben and Amelia started home with the chili pepper. Amelia smiled at all the pretty colors and the cheerful people.

When they reached their building, Amelia took one last look at the market. "Our shopping has been a great success," she said.

"It sure has!" Ben said.

Then Ben and Amelia went inside to tell Dad about their adventure.

The Tianguis

In many neighborhoods in Mexico, there is an open-air market held in the street once a week. This market is called a *tianguis.* Traveling vendors set up stands in the street and sell their wares. Pots, pans, toys, shoes, meat, vegetables—many things can be found at the tianguis!

A tianguis is full of colorful sights and wonderful smells. It is a Mexican tradition. It is also a good way to buy the week's groceries at a good price.

At the end of the day, the sellers take down their stands and pack up their wares. The street is quiet again—until the next week!